Ruchi Gupta

A Reliable and Scalable Multicast Model RSM2

GRIN Verlag

Bibliografische Information der Deutschen Nationalbibliothek:

Die Deutsche Bibliothek verzeichnet diese Publikation in der Deutschen National-
bibliografie; detaillierte bibliografische Daten sind im Internet über http://dnb.d-
nb.de/ abrufbar.

Imprint:

Copyright © 2012 GRIN Verlag GmbH
Druck und Bindung: Books on Demand GmbH, Norderstedt Germany
ISBN: 978-3-656-42448-2

This book at GRIN:

http://www.grin.com/en/e-book/214039/a-reliable-and-scalable-multicast-model-
rsm2

GRIN - Your knowledge has value

Der GRIN Verlag publiziert seit 1998 wissenschaftliche Arbeiten von Studenten, Hochschullehrern und anderen Akademikern als eBook und gedrucktes Buch. Die Verlagswebsite www.grin.com ist die ideale Plattform zur Veröffentlichung von Hausarbeiten, Abschlussarbeiten, wissenschaftlichen Aufsätzen, Dissertationen und Fachbüchern.

Visit us on the internet:

http://www.grin.com/

http://www.facebook.com/grincom

http://www.twitter.com/grin_com

A RELIABLE AND SCALABLE MULTICAST MODEL RSM2

A Thesis Submitted
in Partial Fulfilment of the Requirements
for the Degree of

MASTER OF TECHNOLOGY

in

Computer Science and Engineering

by

Ruchi Gupta

Krishna Engineering College, Ghaziabad

to the

FACULTY OF COMPUTER SCIENCE & ENGINEERING

MAHAMAYA TECHNICAL UNIVERSITY,

NOIDA, INDIA

December, 2012

DECLARATION

I hereby declare that this submission is my own work and that, to the best of my knowledge and belief, it contains no material previously published or written by another person nor material which to a substantial extent has been accepted for the award of any other degree or diploma of the university or other institute of higher learning, except where due acknowledgment has been made in the text.

Signature

Ruchi Gupta

CERTIFICATE

Certified that **Ms. Ruchi Gupta** has carried out the research work presented in this thesis entitled "**A RELIABLE & SCALABLE MULTICAST MODEL (RSM2)**" for the award of **Master of Technology** from **Mahamaya Technical University, Noida** under my supervision. The thesis embodies results of original work, and studies are carried out by the student herself and the contents of the thesis do not form the basis for the award of any other degree to the candidate or to anybody else from this or any other University/Institution.

Place:_____

Date:_____

Mr. Pramod Kumar Sethy

Assistant Professor

ACKNOWLEDGEMENTS

I believe that I would not be able to name everyone separately that they did for me, however, I would like to take the opportunity and express a few words of thanks to my guide, colleagues, friends and family.

Special thanks and gratitude to:

Mr. Pramod Kumar Sethy, Assistant Professor, K.E.C, for accepting me & carrying out research work under him. Your prolonged interest in my work & excellent guidance has shown me a way to pursue excellence & reach my goals. Your cool mind, patience & attitude towards excellence have been a constant source of inspiration for me.

Mr. Rahul Prakash, Assistant Professor, CS-IT Dept., Mewar University, Rajasthan, for your constant support, understanding, help, patience, care, affection and helpful discussions. I am indebted to you from the bottom of my heart.

Sanjiv Kumar, an Engineering Scholar, Mewar University, Rajasthan. I would like to express my best and special thanks for all of your support.

Words are insufficient to express my profound sense of gratitude to my parents & friends, whose encouragement & blessings gave me great physical & moral strength. I would like to thank one of my dearest friends, **Shailendra Jaiswal**, for the valuable support, care and encouragement.

I would like to express my gratitude to the Department of Computer Science & Engineering, Krishna Engineering College, Ghaziabad , that gave me the possibility to complete this thesis.

ABSTRACT

Multicasting is the ability of a communication network to accept a single message from an application and to deliver copies of the message to multiple recipients at different locations. With the emergence of mobile users, many existing Internet-Protocols, including those with multicast support, need to be adapted in order to offer support to this increasingly growing class of users.

Our research in Multicasting, as to design a Multicast Model, which provides reliability & scalability with best path for data delivery. Reliability means guaranteed Delivery of packets. Scalability means capability to serve growing needs .In this context, a few concepts of Proactive-Routing technique are used to make available this model in Infrastructure wireless also. Minimum Spanning path is used to reduce the cost & delay and thus to deliver the packets.

The main characteristic of RSM2 model is, to provide complete multicasting, i.e. at the same time more than one node can act as sender. This model provides one-to-many communications as well as many-to-many communications .The goal of thesis is to design an algorithm describing the function and behavior of Multicast Model (RSM2).

In RSM2 model, Dynamics Manager plays an important role. Dynamics Manager is the specialised Machines, with network computational capabilities. Dynamics Manager is the main focus of this model. Dynamics Manager's functionality makes available this model to work in both wired and wireless networks. Dynamics Managers act as listeners and calculator to perform network computations.

TABLE OF CONTENTS

LIST OF FIGURES

LIST OF TABLES

LIST OF ABBREVIATIONS

ACK	Acknowledgement
Cap_DBuff	Capacity of data buffer
Cap_NBuff	Capacity of NACK_buffer
Comm.	Communication
D_buff	Data buffer
DMs	Dynamic Managers
IGMP	Internet Group Message Protocol
INF	Infinity
NACK	Negative Acknowledgement
N_buff	Buffer for NACK storage
Min_Prio	Minimum Priority given to the edge to be added to Priority Matrix.
Max_Prio	Maximum Priority given to the edge to be added to Priority Matrix
MCPA	Minimum Cost Path Algorithm
OFA	Optimized Flooding Algorithm
RSM2	Reliable & Scalable Multicast Model
RMTP	Reliable & Scalable Multicast Model
RMTP	Reliable Multicast Transport Protocol
T_{emp}	It is the time after which buffer gets empty
T_{init}	It is the value to which priority timer is to be set, initially
T_{store}	It is the time to store the packet
T_{prio}	Priority Timer Based on Priority Matrix
T_{NACK}	It is the time to collect Negative Acknowledgement
TTL	Time to live

CHAPTER - 1   INTRODUCTION

1.1   Background

In the last few years, the Internet has changed from a pure scientific network to the basis of data communication in every-day life. The number of users grows still exponentially and has already reached the order of magnitude of tens of millions. The added spectrum and number of users introduce also new forms of communication into the Internet Communication, not just between two peers, but true group communication. The foundation for the group comm. in the Internet is the IP-multicast service.

Although most of the network connections that were used before multicasting have been known, were *Unicast* (one-to-one) connections. They were basic and can be used for reliable data transmissions back and forth between the two connected nodes. However, these connections are not appropriate for communications from one sender to multiple receivers (one-to-many) or for many senders to many receivers (many-to-many).

Multicast connections, particularly IP Multicast connections, may be more appropriate. IP Multicast connections may be particularly useful for one-to-many communications, as the sender need only transmit data packets once, and multicast enabled routers will copy the packets and send them to joined receivers. As the standard is implemented, there is no need for a sender to generate as many copies of the packets, as the number of receivers.

The need only is to know the Multicast-IP address. Multicasting is the ability of a communication network to accept a single message from an application and to deliver copies of the message to multiple recipients at different locations. Multicasting represents an efficient mechanism that implements point-to-multipoint communications [1].

The two important issues in communication network are: Reliability (guaranteed Delivery) and Scalability (serving growing needs). Our aim to design this model is to deal with these issues. We use Proactive routing in this model, to route the packets. The three basic mechanisms of this

1

Model (RSM2) are neighbour discovery, to discover and maintain connectivity with peers, and constructing minimum spanning path using adjacency matrix.

1.2 Motivation

Reliable multicast is required by many applications such as Multicast File-Transfer, shared white-board, distributed interactive simulation and distributed computing. These applications can potentially have several thousands of participants scattered over a wide area network.

Even though current multicast networks, such as IP multicast networks, provide efficient routing and delivery of packets to groups of receivers based on multicast group addresses, but they are lossy and do not provide the reliability needed by the above applications. Designing scalable approaches and architectures for reliable multicast for an efficient use of both the network and end-host resources, is a challenging task.

Local recovery approaches for reliable multicast, in which a network entity other than the sender aids in error recovery, have potential to provide significant performance gains in terms of reduced bandwidth and delay and higher system throughput. We are using here Receiver-Initiated NACK based Reliable technique and Active-Server based local recovery, to provide reliability & scalability. Another thing that motivates me to design this model is, the nature of nodes to dynamically change their groups[1]. For this purpose, IGMP protocol –II is applied in RSM2. Proactive Routing and combo-casting [1] is used, to make available this model in Dynamic Environment.

1.3 Problem Statement

"TO DESIGN AN ALGORITHM DESCRIBING RSM2 MODEL"

There have been many models and protocols (SRM, RMTP...) have been introduced, to provide reliability and scalability in multicasting communications. The goal of the research is to design an algorithm describing Multicast Model (RSM2), which achieves scalability and reliability. Along with it, our model opt flat approach. The problem with hierarchical approach is that, every time when a receiver becomes the sender, entire hierarchy was changed[4]. The hierarchical

2

Model, RMTP, does not fit in a situation of, where, many nodes can send data simultaneously at same time. Another problem was to choose an effective Designated Receiver, to deliver the packets to all the nodes, under it. Our Multicast Model removes all the above stated problems and provides a cost-effective, delay–effective path to deliver the packets.

1.4   Dissertation Outline

The thesis is organized into seven chapters. The first chapter provides an introduction to the topic being discussed .This chapter gives a brief focus on the background material, studied to complete this work. This thesis is aimed at designing an algorithm, which describes our Multicast Model (RSM2).

The second chapter describes the literature review and related work in the field of Multicasting.

The third chapter describes the work done in this thesis. The work done is divided into 4 sections listing the purpose, general description and working of the Model.

The fourth chapter introduces a proposed algorithm known as MCPA (Minimum Cost-Path Algorithm).

The fifth chapter provides the snapshots after implementation of MCPA algotithm for describing RSM2.

The sixth chapter provides a comparative study of RSM2 with RMTP.

The seventh chapter concludes the thesis and provides recommendations for future work.

3

CHAPTER - 2   LITERATURE REVIEW

2.1 Multicasting

MULTICASTING provides an effective and efficient way of disseminating data from a sender to a group of receivers. Instead of sending a separate copy of the data to each individual receiver, the sender just sends a single copy to all the receivers. A multicast tree is set up in the network with sender at the root node and the receivers at the leaf nodes. Data generated by the sender flows through the multicast tree, traversing each tree edge exactly once [4]. However, distribution of data using the multicast tree in an unreliable network does not guarantee reliable delivery, which is the prime requirement for several important applications, such as distribution of software, financial information, electronic newspapers, billing records, and medical images [4].

2.2 What is Multicast?

Normal IP packets are sent from a single source to a single recipient. Along the way these packets are forwarded by a number of routers between the source and recipient, according to forwarding table information that has been built up by configuration and routing protocol activity. This form of IP packet delivery is known as **unicast.**

However, some scenarios (for example, audio/video streaming broadcasts) need individual IP packets to be delivered to multiple destinations. Sending multiple unicast packets to achieve this is unacceptable because it would require the source to hold a complete list of recipients. Multiple identical copies of the same data would flow over the same links, increasing bandwidth requirements and costs. Instead, data to multiple destinations can be delivered using multicast.

Multicast allows the source to send a single copy of data, using a single address for the entire group of recipients. Routers between the source and recipients use the group address to route the data. The routers forward duplicate data packets wherever the path to recipients diverges.

4

A multicast group identifies a set of recipients that are interested in a particular data stream, and is represented by an IP address from a well-defined range. Data addressed to this IP address is forwarded to all members of the multicast group.

A source host sends data to a multicast group by simply setting the destination IP address of the datagram to be the multicast group address. Sources do not need to register in any way before they can begin sending data to a group, and do not need to be members of the group themselves.

In the following diagram, S2 sends a single copy of its multicast data addressed to the multicast group. The group consists of hosts G1, G2 and G3. The data is duplicated at routers R1 and R3 to ensure that it reaches all the hosts that are interested in this multicast data. G4 and G5 do not belong to the multicast group, and hence do not receive copies of the data.

In the diagram as shown below,

- S indicates a host sending multicast data
- G indicates a host which may or may not be a member of the multicast group
- R indicates a multicast-capable router.

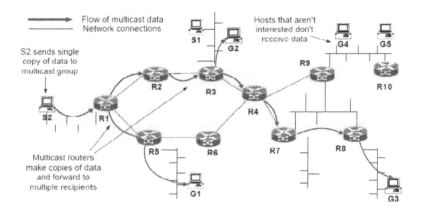

Figure 2.1 Overview of Multicasting

Information about which parts of the network contain members of a particular multicast group is distributed as follows.

Hosts who wish to receive data from the multicast group join the group by sending a message to a multicast router on a local interface, using a multicast group membership discovery protocol such as IGMP or MLD.

- ❖ Multicast traffic reaches all of the recipients that have joined the multicast group

- ❖ Multicast traffic does not reach networks that do not have any such recipients (unless the network is a transit network on the way to other recipients)

- ❖ The number of identical copies of the same data flowing over the same link is minimized.

To satisfy these requirements, multicast routing protocols calculate a multicast distribution tree of recipients.

6

2.3 How to Define Cost of the link

There are various factors, on the basis of which, cost of a link is defined. These factors include Bandwidth, delay, throughput (no. of packets lost) etc. If a link has high cost, it means, it has less efficiency and will cause more packets to be lost. So, our approach is to use kruskal's algorithm, which choose the links of least-cost, to transmit the packet from sender to receiver(s).

2.4 Minimum Spanning Tree

A tree is a connected (undirected) graph with no cycles.

Given an undirected and connected graph $G = (V, E)$, a spanning tree of G is a sub graph

$G' = (V', E')$ of G such that

I.   G' is a tree, and

II. $V' = V$

If the graph G is weighted, then a minimum spanning tree (MST) of G has the smallest edge-weight sum among all spanning trees of G. Note that when all the edges of the graph have distinct weights, the MST is unique. If $V = \{v0, v1... vi, vj\}$, then the MST has $n - 1$ edges.

These edges must be chosen among potentially $n (n - 1)/2$ candidates. This gives a lower bound on the number of operations required to compute the MST since each edge must be examined at least once.

For convenience, we henceforth refer to the weight of edge (vi, vj) as the distance separating vi and vj and denote it by $dist(vi, vj)$. We are using this approach , because, it helps in reduction the traffic. Since, the packet will follow only the spanning path.

Kruskal's Algorithm (G, w)

Step 1. A←φ

Step 2. for each vertex v€V [G]

Step 3. do MAKE-SET(v)

Step 4. Sort the edges of E into non-decreasing order by weight 'w'

Step 5. for each edge (u,v)€ E , taken in non-decreasing order by weight.

Step 6. do if FIND-SET (u) ≠FIND-SET(v)

Step 7. then A←AU{(u,v)}

Step 8. Union (u, v)

2.5   Ack-Implosion Problem

For a reliable multicasting, every receiver send acknowledgements back to the sender and it is difficult to provide scalability to large numbers of receivers. In this way, for large number of receivers, there could be lack of acknowledgement-packets returning to the sender for every packet that it transmits. Although, using a specialized protocol that very fewer acknowledgements than TCP can still cause an ACK implosion whenever a packet is lost during transmission because every receiver would notify the sender of the missing packet.

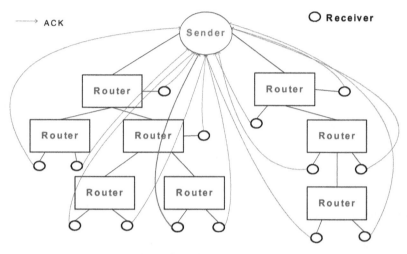

Figure 2.2 Ack-implosion Problem

2.6 IGMP

The following describes the basic operation of IGMP, common to all versions. Note that a multicast router acts as both an IGMP host and an IGMP router in this and following descriptions, and as a result can respond to its own IGMP messages.

❖ If a host wishes to join a new multicast group, it sends an unsolicited IGMP Report message for that group.

❖ A local router picks up the IGMP Report message and uses a multicast routing   protocol to join the multicast group.

❖ Periodically, a special router called the Querier broadcasts IGMP Query messages onto the LAN to check which groups the local hosts are subscribed to.

❖ Hosts respond to the Query messages by sending IGMP Report messages   indicating their group memberships.

All routers on the LAN receive the Report messages and note the memberships of   hosts on the LAN. If a router does not receive a Report message for a particular   group for a period of time, the router assumes there are no more members of the   group on the LAN, and removes itself from the multicast group.

Note that all IGMP messages are raw IP datagram, and are sent to multicast group addresses, with a TTL of 1. Since raw IP does not provide reliable transport, some messages are sent multiple times to aid reliability.

Sending Group Membership Queries

Only one router sends IGMP Query messages onto a particular LAN. This router is called the Querier. IGMPv1 depended on the multicast routing protocol to decide which router was the Querier. IGMPv2 introduced a Querier election process, which works as follows.

By default, a router takes the role of Querier. If a Querier receives an IGMP Query message from a router on the same interface and with a lower IP address, it stops being the Querier. If a router has stopped being the Querier, but does not receive an IGMP Query message within a configured interval, it becomes the Querier again.

Responding to Group Membership Queries

Ordinary LAN routers typically forward multicast traffic onto all other LAN segments. Therefore, the Querier does not need to know exactly which hosts on the LAN require data for a particular multicast group. It only needs to know that one host requires the multicast data.

To avoid a 'storm' of responses to an IGMP Query message, each host that receives this message starts a randomized timer for each group that it is a member of. When this timer pops, the host sends an IGMP Report message, which is addressed to that group. Any other hosts that are members of the group also receive the message, at which point they cancel their timer for the group. This mechanism ensures that at most one IGMP Report message is sent for each multicast group in response to a single Query.

IGMPv2 introduced a Leave Group message, which is sent by a host when it leaves a multicast group for which it was the last host to send an IGMP Report message. Receipt of this message causes the Querier possibly to reduce the remaining lifetime of its state for the group, and to send a group-specific IGMP Query message to the multicast group.

Note that the Leave Group message in not used with IGMPv3, as its source address filtering mechanism provides the same functionality.

2.7   Flooding Vs. Broadcasting

Flooding is the first strategy that comes to our mind in the reference of multicasting. In this technique, a router receives a packet and, without even looking at the destination group address, sends it out from every interface except the one from which it was received. Flooding accomplishes the first goal of multicasting [6], i.e. "Every Network with active members receives the packet"

But the problem with Flooding is: it creates loops. A packet that has left the router may come back again from another interface or the same interface and forwarded again. So, one solution to this problem is, to keep, a copy of the packet for a while and discards any duplicates to prevent loops formation.

Flooding algorithm is guaranteed to find and utilize the shortest path for sending packets because it naturally uses every path in the network. There are no complexities in this routing algorithm; it is very easy to implement.

Of course, there are few disadvantages of the flooding algorithm as well. Because packets are sent through every outgoing link, the bandwidth is obviously wasted. This means flooding can actually degrade the reliability of a computer network.

Unless necessary precautions like hop count or time to live are taken, duplicate copies can circulate within the network without stopping. One of the possible precautions is to ask nodes to track each packet passing through it and make sure that a packet goes through it only once.

Another precaution is called selective flooding. In Selective flooding, nodes may forward packets only in the (approximately) correct direction [7].

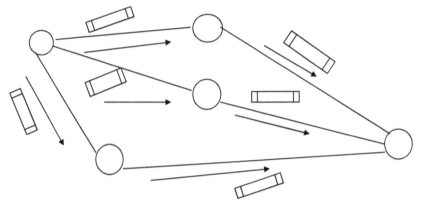

Figure 2.3 Flooding on the network

In Broadcast communication, One-to-all relationship exists between the source and the destinations. It means, there is only one source host but all others are destination hosts. Broadcasting is a method used in computer networking, which makes sure that every device in the network will receive a (broadcasted) packet [7]. The Internet does not explicitly support broadcasting because of the huge amount of traffic that, it would create and because of the bandwidth that, it would need.

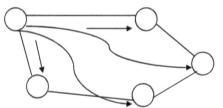

Figure 2.4 Broadcasting on Network

How Flooding is different from Broadcasting?

Sending a packet to all hosts simultaneously is broadcasting. But flooding does not send packets to all the hosts simultaneously. The packets would ultimately reach all nodes in the network due

12

to flooding. Flooding may send the same packet along the same link multiple times, but broadcasting sends a packet along a link at most once. Several copies of the same packet may reach nodes in flooding, while broadcasting does not cause that problem. Unlike flooding, broadcasting is done by specifying a special broadcast address on packets [7].

2.8   Various Approaches to Reliable Multicasting

Any reliable multicast protocol requires some recovery mechanism. A generic description of a recovery mechanism consists of a prioritized list of recovery servers/receivers (clients), hierarchically and/or geographically and/or randomly organized. Recovery requests are sent to the recovery clients on the list one-by-one until the recovery effort is successful. There are many recovery strategies available in literature fitting the generic description [3].

2.8.1   SRM

Scalable Reliable Multicast (SRM) [8] is a simple and robust retransmission-based protocol. SRM uses IP multicast to multicast messages to all the members of the reliable multicast group. In turn, IP multicast uses underlying spanning trees to disseminate these messages to all group members in a best-effort manner, i.e., with no delivery or performance guarantees. Packet recovery in SRM is initiated when a receiver detects a loss and schedules the transmission of a request; an error control message requesting the retransmission of the missing packet. If a request for the same packet is received prior to the transmission of this local request, then the local request is rescheduled by performing an exponential back-off. When a group member receives a request for a packet that it has already received, the group member schedules a reply; a retransmission of the requested packet. If a reply for the same packet is received prior to the transmission of this local reply, then the local reply is cancelled. Using this scheme, all session members participate in the packet recovery process and share the associated overhead. SRM minimizes duplicate error control and retransmission traffic through deterministic and probabilistic suppression. These suppression techniques prescribe how requests and replies should be scheduled so that only few requests and replies are transmitted for each loss. Deterministic suppression prescribes that request and reply scheduling timers be set proportionately to the distance from the source and the requestor, respectively. Thus, the requests of ancestors suppress those of their descendants. Probabilistic suppression prescribes that

13

members that are equidistant from the source and the requestor probabilistically vary the scheduling times of their requests and replies, respectively. Thus, sibling requestor and replier hosts are afforded the opportunity to suppress each other. Unfortunately, suppression introduces a trade-off between the number of duplicate requests and replies and the recovery latency — the scheduling of requests and replies must be delayed sufficiently so as to minimize the number of duplicate requests and replies [8].

2.8.2 RMTP

RMTP[4] is based on a hierarchical structure in which receivers are grouped into local regions or domains and in each domain there is a special receiver called a designated receiver (DR), which is, responsible for sending acknowledgments periodically to the sender, for processing acknowledgment from receivers in its domain, and for retransmitting lost packets to the corresponding receivers. Since lost packets are recovered by local retransmissions as opposed to retransmissions from the original sender, end-to-end latency is significant reduced, and the overall throughput is improved as well. Also, since only the DR's send their acknowledgments to the sender, instead of all receivers sending their acknowledgments to the sender, a single acknowledgment is generated per local region and this prevents acknowledgment implosion. Receivers in RMTP send their acknowledgments to the DR's periodically, thereby simplifying error recovery. In addition, lost packets are recovered by selective repeat retransmissions, leading to improved throughput at the cost of minimal additional buffering at the receivers [4].

2.8.3 Light-weight Reliable Multicast Protocol

LRMP provides a minimum set of functions for end-to-end reliable multicast network transport suitable for bulk data transfer to multiple receivers. LRMP is designed to work in heterogeneous network environments and support multiple data senders. A totally distributed control scheme is adopted for local error recovery so that no prior configuration and no router support are required. Subgroups are formed implicitly and have no group leaders. Packet loss is reported upon a random timeout first to the lowest level subgroup, then to a higher subgroup and so on until it is repaired. This simple scheme is rather efficient in duplicate NACK and repair suppression [2].

CHAPTER - 3   SYSTEM DESIGN

3.1 Design Objectives

The design of RSM2 is motivated by the local recovery scheme of RMTP and other existing reliable multicast protocols. RSM2 is intended to take advantages from the existing protocols and avoid their drawbacks. The model has been designed in order to meet the top level goals which must be met at very first stage. Since, many of reliable multicast issues are still under research; some second level goals are established and are expected to be fully met at the second stage.

In the Internet environment, hosts are generally interconnected via heterogeneous links and dispersed world-wide. The quality of service of their network links such as the bandwidth and packet propagation time varies from one to another. The primary goal is thus to provide a reliable data delivery service over such a heterogeneous environment [2].The goals of RSM2 are summarized as follows:

- It must ensure reliable data delivery.

- It must scale well to large group of users.

- It must continue to work for majority of receivers, even in case where some receivers may leave their group, or some new receivers join the group, during the transmission.

- It must provide reasonable performance.

- It must work in Infrastructured wireless networks.

3.2 Different Multicasting Scenarios

There are three different scenarios can be seen in multicasting communications:

1. Multicasting in Tight-coupled scenario: This type of scenario can be seen in RMTP, where the members cannot leave or join the group, during the communication. The position of the members is static.

2. Multicasting in loosely-coupled scenario: In this scenario, the members can join or leave the group at any time or at any location. So, the control of data-transmission depends upon the behaviour of majority of receivers. LRMP works in this scenario.

3. Multicasting in Mix-scenario: It is the combination of dynamic and statics. RSM2 is designed to work in this scenario.

3.3 RSM2 Architecture and Assumptions

RSM2 is based on flat architecture. Let all the nodes in the network are connected with each other, through local area switches or routers. These routers are collocated with Dynamics Manager (DM).The assumptions made in the design of model is as follows:

1. Active Server Based Local Recovery: It makes use of specially designated hosts that have all the network- computational ability, known as Dynamics Manager (DM).
2. Dynamics Manager: DMs are collocated with each router of the network. They have the entire essential network computational ability likes – to maintain a proper data of the nodes that are linked with it, to compute a Partial_cost_ matrix, and to assign a priority.
3. Cost Matrix: In a Heterogeneous environment, it is not possible that all links are alike. Hence, on the basis of their property we assign a cost to each link. Cost matrix shows the cost associated with each link.
   If there is no link between any two nodes, in that case, matrix assigns the cost as infinity.
4. Priority Matrix: In the model, priority matrix is designed from the cost matrix. To send the packets, the path is decided on the basis of priority matrix.
5. Echo packet: Whenever a node wants to send the data to others, then sender first sends an echo packet. In that packet , there are two fields :
   a. Group-id: It indicates the group to whom sender wants to communicate.
   b. Sender-id: It defines the address of the sender.

Echo packet as moves through the network, it stores the information about path and cost.

6. Response Packet: This packet is sent by DM, to the sender, in response to Echo Packet.

7. IGMP drive: As the Echo packet received by the DMs, they run IGMP protocol, to know the group status of the nodes under them. This report is forwarded to their neighbouring DMs. These reports make the DMs up-to-date always. Also, DMs periodically run IGMP protocol and send the status report to others.

8. NACK –Based Combo-Casting Approach: Since, each data packet has a unique sequence number. Hence, if a packet is missed by a node, it sends a NACK to the DM. DM do not retransmits that packet immediately. As the DM gets an ACK / NACK for the last packet, DM analyses NACKs. On the basis of no. of NACKs, DM decides to retransmit the packet by unicasting or multicasting.

9. Buffer Management: Each DM has two buffers, one buffer for data packets, and another buffer for NACKs .Initially, the buffer capacity is assumed to be unlimited. But, the capacity is confined, as the first packet is received.

3.3.1 Flat Design of RSM2

RSM2 opts Flat structure .The aim to work with flat structure, is to remove the restrictions with hierarchical design. Flat Design of RSM2 model facilitates us to overcome from following difficulties:

- The problem with hierarchical approach is that, every time when a receiver becomes the sender, entire hierarchy was changed.

- The hierarchical Model, RMTP, does not fit in a situation of, where, many nodes can send data simultaneously at same time. Because, when we create hierarchy, the root is only one that is the sender. But if many senders start to send data, then multiple roots can be possible. RMTP does not provide the solution for such kind of situations.

3.3.2 Structure of an Echo Packet

The Echo Packet comprises of two fields:

17

1. Sender_id: It defines the address of the sender.

2. Group_id: It indicates the Group_id, to whom the sender wants to communicate.

ESeq_No	Sender_id	Group_id

Figure 3.1 Structure of an Echo-Packet

3.3.3 Structure of the Data Packet

The data packet comprises of four fields:

1. Seq_No. : This field provides a unique identity to the packet. If the packet is missed by a receiver node, then it sends a NACK for the packet with this Seq_no.
2. Path: Sender creates a path-vector using priority matrix. This Path-vector is specified in the field of path and the data packet is sent through this path.
3. MORE (m): In each packet, the last field either sets to 'm' or to 'e'.
    3.1 If the last field sets to 'm': This field indicates how many packets will be sent after this packet.
    3.2 If the last field sets to 'e': It indicates, it is the last packet of this session.
4. Priority: if the value of Priority is low, means lesser cost, hence for each incoming packet, DM will buffers the packet and starts the timer. As T_{prio} gets out, packet will be dropped and buffer gets emptied.
5. Data : the data to be transmit

DSeq_No.	Path	MORE (m) /END (e).	Priority	Data

Figure 3.2 Structure of Data- Packet

18

3.3.4 BUFFER MANAGEMENT

We are introducing a new approach for buffer management .First thing; each DM maintains two buffers as follows:

1. Data buffer: The buffer stores the entire data packet to send, and do not get empty immediately. The buffer is emptied after T_{prio} gets stop.
2. Nack_buffer: This buffer stores the NACKs, received from receiver nodes. Since, NACKs are not served immediately; hence, we need this buffer.

Buffer is considered as a stack with unlimited capacity. Second thing is to estimate Buffer capacity. As, DMs get first data packet, they estimate their buffer-size .Since, in first data packet, it is indicated, how many packets will be sent after this first packet. Capacity of the buffer is defined in terms of no. of slots.

No. of slots in D_buff = No. of packets being transmit.

Cap_DBuff = Cap_Nbuff

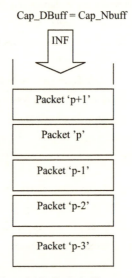

Figure 3.3 Buffer looks like as a stack

19

DMs buffers all the incoming packets .Since this model opts , NACK-based error-recovery scheme , hence , in case , as first NACK is obtained for the particular packet 'p', then, DMs will serve these NACKs using combo-casting algorithm.

3.3.5 Management of NACK Buffer

Dynamic Manager first stores all the NACKS, and wait for a random amount of time. As the time gets out, DMs decide either to retransmit the data through multicasting or via unicasting. If more NACKs are received for the same packet then DM subgroups them into a new group and multicast the missed data-packet. In case, there is one or two nodes, send NACK for the same packet then DMs unicast the missed data packet.

3.3.6 DYNAMICS MANAGER

In RSM2 model, Dynamics Manager plays an important role. Dynamics Manager is the specialised Machines, with network computational capabilities. Dynamics Manager is the main focus of this model. Dynamics Manager's functionality makes available this model to work in both wired and wireless networks. Dynamics Managers act as listeners and calculator to perform network computations.

The importance of Dynamics Manager is described as follows:

- Sends Status report periodically or at topology's update.
- Create Partial Matrix: Dynamics Manager on receiving the echo packet or getting the topology-updates, create the matrix .This matrix has the information of those nodes that are directly connected with this DM. Hence, this matrix is called Partial-Matrix.
- Calculate Priority of the link: Dynamics Manager calculates the priority matrix from the work matrix using the Priority Constraint, as follows :

$$P[i][j] = \{ \; Exclude \, Edge(i,j), if \; \forall (i,j) \in E \; forms \, loop$$
$$otherwise, Assign \Pr iority \; \forall (i,j) \}$$

Priority Matrix ()

{

```
for (i=1; i<=n; i++)
    {
    for (j=1; j<=2; j++)
        {
        if (W[i] [j] == Least_cost)
            {
                P[i] [j]  ←  Min_Prio;
            }
        else(C[i] [j] == High_cost)
            {
                P[i] [j]  ←  Max._prio;
            }
    }
```

- Set the Priority Timer: The Priority matrix is used to set the priority timer. Since the packet already contains the path and priority of each path. DMs gets the priority for the path, through which packet will reach to destination via DM(s). If DM finds the link has lower priority-value then T_{prio} will be in function for small unit of time. Since, the link has low cost and having less chances to miss the data, if passes through this link. So, as the T_{prio} gets out. Data will be emptied out of the buffer.

Priority Timer ()
    {

//Assume that if a link (connects two nodes-A and B) has least cost, then initially the timer is initialised to 10ns.

T_{init} = 10ns;

p = priority assigned to the edge

for(i=1; p<=i; i++)
    {
    $T_{prio.}$ = i* T_{init};
    }
    }

21

- Buffering for the incoming packets: DMs use two kinds of Buffers.
  1. Data buffer: The buffer stores the entire data packet to send, and do not get empty immediately. The buffer is emptied, after T_{prio} stops.
  2. Nack_buffer: This buffer stores the NACKs, received from receiver nodes. Since, NACKs are not served immediately, hence, we need this buffer.
- NACK –maintenance: RSM2 model's special feature is, it provides a separate buffer for Nack. Dynamic Manager first stores all the NACKS, and wait for a random amount of time, T_{NACK}. As, the time gets out, DMs retransmit the data via combo-casting.

3.4   General Description

3.4.1   DESCRIPTION OF THE MODEL (RSM2)

RSM2 Model is designed to work in both kind of environment, either it is wired or it is wireless .Let us study our Model in details.

3.4.1.1   Optimized Flooding Algorithm (OFA)

In this model, we use flooding technique, but it has been optimized to overcome the drawbacks of Flooding. Each packet has a sequence no. When the DM gets the packet, starts T_{stores} timer for t_{store} time. As the t_{store} time gets out, DM drops the packet, but save its seq. No for ($2\ t_{store}$) some time. It prevents looping. As DM receives the same packet or packet with same sequence number, then DM will discard it and not floods to the network. As, the DM gets updated information regarding packet or topology's change, then it immediately floods to the network.

22

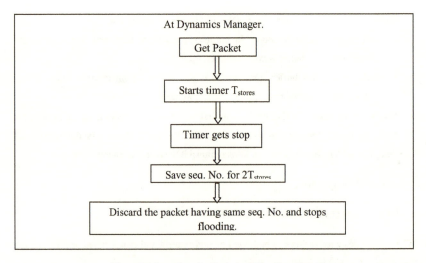

Figure 3.4 Procedure for Optimized Flooding Algorithm

3.4.1.2 NACK Based Packet Recovery

RSM2 model opts NACK-Based packet recovery. The recipient will not acknowledge the DM(s) or sender for each received packet. It prevents the ACK-implosion problem. If sender misses a packet, then immediately send NACK for it. As DM gets NACK, will not serve immediately, wait for a random amount of time, and after that serves the request using Combo-casting. There are three possibilities, that is being discussed below:

Possible Case-I:

As, the receiver missed the packet, it sends the NACK immediately. So, if NACK for Packet-5 comes to DM then it acknowledges the receipt of all the packets, sent before packet-5.

Possible Case-II:

DMs receive a request for that packet, which has been emptied out the buffer. In that case, DMs will wait for a random amount of time, and then sends this request to the receivers under them. If receiver (under DM) get that packet, will serve the request.

Otherwise DMs will flood this request to other DMs, using optimized flooding. In case, no one can serve this request, only then, the request will go to the sender.

Possible Case-III:

As, the receiver gets the last packet of the sequence, it sends an Over-packet to DM. This packet acknowledges that, all the packets have been received successfully.

3.4.1.3 Need To Modify Packet Structure and Buffering

Dynamics Manager is the main focus of this model. Dynamics Manager's functionality makes available this model to work in both wired and wireless networks. As DMs use two kinds of Buffers:

1. Data_buffer: The buffer stores the entire data packet to send, and do not get empty immediately. The buffer is emptied, after $T_{prio.}$ Stops.
2. Nack_buffer: This buffer stores the NACKs, received from receiver nodes. Since, NACKs are not served immediately; hence, we need this buffer.

Since, after the priority path formation, some information is added to the header of the packet, discussed below. This information is used further in path maintenance and buffer maintenance.

1. Dseq_No: it is the sequence number, which is added to the packet, to distinguish it from others, and to assemble in proper order.
2. Path: this field contains the path, through which packet goes to the recipients. DMs will forward to next node, using this path.
3. More (m) /End (e): In each packet, the last field either sets to 'm' or to 'e'.
    3.1. If the last field sets to 'm': This field indicates how many packets will be sent after this packet.
    3.2. If the last field sets to 'e': It indicates, it is the last packet of this session.
4. Priority: if the value of Priority is low, means lesser cost, hence for each incoming packet, DM will buffers the packet and starts. As T_{prio} gets out, packet will be dropped and buffer get emptied.

24

3.4.1.4 Priority Timer

The designing of Priority timer is based on Priority matrix. If the path has low cost, then it also has low priority. Then, for the low-cost path, the T_{prio} will be set to small time units. As the T_{prio} gets out, the buffer will be emptied.

For the high-cost path, the T_{prio} will be set to large time units. As the T_{prio} gets stop, the buffer will be emptied. In case the T_{prio} gets out and then, NACK comes for the Packet, then it will be served by its predecessor node or successor node. It might be the possibility, if no one can serve that request, then that request is served by sender directly.

3.4.1.5 Minimizing Congestion due to Error

RSM2 model reduces the congestion due to packet-retransmission. Since, we have introduced a new approach of NACK-buffer to fulfil NACK-Based recovery.

Dynamic Manager first stores all the NACKS, and wait for a random amount of time, T_{NACK}. As, the time gets out DMs retransmit the data via combo-casting.

3.4.1.6 Computations for Minimum-Cost Path

For computing the minimum-cost path we use Kruskal's algorithm that i have discussed in second chapter.

3.4.1.7 Combo-Casting

Dynamic Managers first stores all the NACKS, and wait for a random amount of time, T_{NACK}. As the time gets out DMs decide either to retransmit the data through multicasting or via unicasting. If more NACKs are received for the same packet then DM subgroups them into a new group and multicast the missed data-packet. In case, there is one or two nodes send NACK for the same packet, then, DMs unicast the missed data packet.

Procedure Combo-casting ( )
{
t_{NACK} ⟵ Storage time for NACKs.

25

```
while ( t_NACK >0)
    {
    do nothing , only stores the packet ;
    }
    if (i<=2)
        {
            Unicast()
            {
            Transmit the data via unicasting ;
            }
        else {
            Multicasting()
            {
            Transmit the data via multicasting;
            }
}
```

3.4.2   Working of the Model

Step 1. Sender node floods an ECHO packet, using optimized flooding algorithm. This Packet stores the path, as it moves.

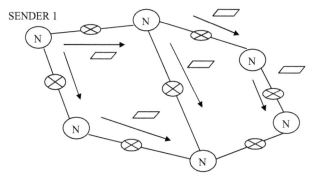

Figure 3.5 Echo packet flows throughout the network using Optimized Flooding Algorithm

Step 2. In response to the received ECHO packet, DMs, construct a cost matrix. The cost matrix will be of nxn, 'n' is the no. of nodes, in connection with DMs, directly.

$$C[i][j] = \begin{pmatrix} C_{11} & \cdots & C_{1n} \\ \vdots & \ddots & \vdots \\ C_{n1} & \cdots & C_{nn} \end{pmatrix}$$

Step 3. This Cost matrix is flooded to all the DMs. If DMs sees any new report, modifies their report. Otherwise discard it. Since, every report has unique sequence number, which is updated at each change

Step 4. The final cost matrix is created at the sender. Sender Choose a DM for further Network computations.

Step 5. The DM will take cost matrix and runs steps-4 to 8 of MCPA algorithm.

Step 6. At the sender site , step-9 of MCPA algorithm is executed.

Step 7. The data-packet is delivered through the minimum-cost Data path, as formed in above step (6).

CHAPTER - 4   PROPOSED ALGORITHM: MCPA

4.1   Basis for the Proposed Algorithm – MCPA (Minimum Cost - Path Algorithm)

- DESIGN OF COST MATRIX

  The cost matrix is designed to define the cost between each pair of nodes, with the following cost constraint:

  $$C[i][j] = \{INFINITY, iff\ (i,j) \notin E \vee (\forall(i,j), i = j$$
  $$otherwise, Assign\ Cost\}$$

- DESIGN OF WORK MATRIX

  The work matrix is designed to define the priority to the edges, with the following work constraint:

  $$W[i][j] = \{\ Leave\ Edge(i', j'), if\ i = j' \wedge j = i', \forall(i,j) \wedge (i', j') \in E$$
  $$otherwise, Include\ Edge(i', j')\}$$

- DESIGN OF PRIORITY MATRIX

  The priority matrix is designed to define the priority to the edges, with the following priority constraint:

  $$P[i][j] = \{\ Exclude\ Edge(i, j), if\ \forall(i, j) \in E\ forms\ loop$$
  $$otherwise, Assign\ \Pr iority\ \forall(i, j)\}$$

- DESIGN OF DATA-PATH

  The data delivery path is designed to deliver the data to the desirable recipient's. Desirable recipients belong to the specific group(s), to whom Sender wants to communicate.

  $$Data\ path \longleftarrow Choose\ (u,v) \in \{specific\ group(s)\}.(u,v) \in E.$$

- COMBO-CASTING

  Dynamic Managers first stores all the NACKs, and wait for a random amount of time, T_{NACK}. As, the time gets out DMs decide either to retransmit the data through multicasting or via unicasting. If more NACKs are received for the same packet then DM subgroups them into a new group and multicast the missed data-packet. In case, there is one or two nodes send NACK for the same packet, then, DMs unicast the missed data packet.

- PRIORITY TIMER MANAGEMENT

The Priority matrix is used to set the priority timer. Since the packet already contains the path and priority of each path. DMs gets the priority for the path, through which packet will reach to destination via DM(s). If DM finds the link has lower priority-value, and then T_{prio} will be in function for small unit of time. Since, the link has low cost and having less chances to miss the data, if passes through this link. So, as the T_{prio} gets out data will be emptied out of the buffer.

- OPTIMIZED FLOODING ALGORITHM (OFA)

When the DM gets the packet, starts T_{stores} timer for t_{store} time. As the t_{store} time gets out, DM drops the packet, but save its seq. No for (2 t_{store}) some time. It prevents looping. As DM receives the same packet or packet with same sequence number, then DM will discard it and not floods to the network.

As, the DM gets updated information regarding packet or topology's change, then it immediately floods to the network.

Procedure OFA()

{

   // T_{store} ◄— time to store the packet.

    Step 1.   DM◄—getpacket();

    Step 2.   pck ◄— no. of packets to be send in one session.

    Step 3.   For (i=1;i<=pck;i++)

          {

          T_{store} = 20ns. // assume each incoming packet will be stored in buffer for 20ns, first .

            While ($T_{store} > 0$)

              {

            Stores the packet;

            if (Packet$_{in}$ ==Packet$_{store}$)

              {

29

Discard the packet

Stop flooding ;

}

Else

{

store the packet

forward to connected node except that from which it come;

}

}

}

Step 4.   Drop the packet;

Step 5.   Save the sequence no;

Step 6.   If (seq_noPacket$_{in}$ == seq_noPacket$_{empty}$)

Discard the packet;

Step 7.   Else store the packet and Go to Step-3.

4.1.1   Proposed Algorithm for RSM2 –MCPA

MCPA (Minimum Cost-Path Algorithm)

Procedure()

{

// d ← no. of Dynamics Managers.

// E ← set of edges.

// S ← set of senders.

// n ← No. of nodes.

Step 1.   Sender sends ECHO-packet.

Step 2.   DMs forms partial-cost matrix.

30

```
Create_partial_matrix()

    {

    For ( i=1 ; i<=n; i++)

        {

        For (j=1; j<=n ;j++)

            {

                If  (i==j OR  No edge between i and j)

                C[i][j] ← INF ;

            else

                C[i][j] ← Cost of the link ;

            }

        }

    }
```

Step 3.   flood_partial_ matrix()

```
    {

        for( i=1;i<=d; i++)

            {

                While (next_node is not sender)

                    {

                    Next_node  ←  Partial-Cost Matrix;
```

31

}

}　}

Step 3.1. If topology ⟵ updates

Step 3.2. Else

Go to step 4.

Step 4.　Sender constructs the final cost matrix using, the Partial-Cost matrix.

Step 5.　Final cost matrix is given to a chosen DM. Choice depends on what criteria (cost, distance .....etc.) is selected by the sender.

Step 6.　At Dynamics Manager's site :

Step 6.1. Work-Matrix is created using Cost-Matrix , with following work-constraint.

$$W[i][j] = \{ \, Leave\,Edge\,(i',j'), if\ i=j' \wedge j=i', \ \forall(i,j) \wedge (i',j') \in E$$
$$otherwise, Include\,Edge(i',j') \}$$

for (i=1; i<=n; i++)

　　{

　　for (j=1 ; j<=2 ;j++)

　　{

　　i　⟵No. of edges;

　　j1　⟵Connected Edge;

　　j2　⟵Cost to edge;

　　}

　　}

Step 6.2. Heap Sort the Work Matrix on the basis of cost.

Step 6.3. Create the priority matrix, with following Priority constraint:

$$P[i][j] = \{ \, Exclude\,Edge(i,j), if\ \forall(i,j) \in E\ forms\ loop$$
$$otherwise, Assign \Pr iority\ \forall(i,j) \}$$

for (i=1; i<=n; i++)

　　{

　　for (j=1 ; j<=2 ;j++)

　　{

32

Create the priority matrix

If (W[i][j] ==Least_cost)

P[i][j]   ←Min_Prio;

Else (C[i][j]==High_cost)

P[i][j]   ← Max._prio;

}

}

Step 6.4. The priority matrix is sent to Sender.

Step 7.   At Sender :

Create Data Delivery path using Priority Matrix.

Data path ←— Choose (u,v) ∈ {specific group(s)}.(u,v) ∈ E.

Step 8.   Packet is created and forwarded according to the path mentioned in header of the packet

Step 8.1. DMs run Priority Timer() algorithm for Data-buffer maintenance on the basis of priority.

Priority Timer()

{//Assume that if a link (connects two nodes-A and B) has least cost, then initially the timer is initialised to 10ns}

T_{init} = 10ns;

p = priority assigned to the edge

for(i=1; p<=i; i++)

{

$T_{prio.}$ = i* T_{init};

}

}

Step 8.2. DMs run Combo-casting algo() for NACK-serving.

If(NACK received before the buffer empties the missed packet)

{

Procedure Combo-casting( )

{

t_{NACK} ←—   Storage time for NACKs.

33

```
                    while ( t_NACK >0)
                        {
                    do nothing , only stores the NACK ;
                        }
                    if (i<=2)
                        {
                    Unicast()
                        {
                    Transmit the data via unicasting;
                        }
            else
                {
            Multicasting()
                {
            Transmit the data via multicasting;
        }
      }
    }
else
{
DMs will flood that request to all DMs, and set its timer TNACK.
If time gets out and no packet receives, then DM will send NACK to
    Original Sender directly.
else go to step- 8.1.
      }
    }
} //END
```

4.1.1.1   Analysis of MCPA Algorithm

The Speciality of this algorithm is, as we go forward, our data get more filtered and consolidated. In this way, we remove unnecessary data-traffic to create and prevent from congestion on network. The data is delivered via minimum-cost path safely and reliably, to desirable recipients.

The efficiency of an algorithm can be measured by inserting a counter in the algorithm in order to count the number of times the basic operation is executed. This is straightforward method of counting an efficiency of algorithm.

Table 4.1 Complexity analysis for MCPA algorithm

The frequency count is a count that denotes how many times the particular statement is executed. We are using "FREQUENCY COUNT" method to analyse the algorithm MCPA, designed for RSM2 Model.

STEPS	OPERATIONS	FREQUENCY_COUNTS
1.	Echo – operation (By sender)	$C(n) = O(1)$ i.e. constant
2.	Partal_Cost_Matrix Construction (By Dynamics Manager)	$C(n) = \sum_{i=1}^{n}\sum_{i=1}^{n} 1$; where, $n=2$. $= \sum_{i=1}^{n} 2 = O(4)$
3.	Flood_Partial_Cost_Matrix (By Dynamics Manager)	$C(n) = \sum_{i=1}^{d}(k+1)$
4.	Final_Cost_matrix Construction (By Sender)	$C(n) = O(n^2)$
5.	Selection of DM (Sender Site)	$C(n) = O(1)$ i.e. constant
6.	AT DM's site Step 6.1 Work_Matrix construction Step 6.2 Heap Sort Step 6.3 Priority Matrix Construction Step 6.4 Priority Matrix sent to sender	$C(n) = \sum_{i=1}^{n}\sum_{i=1}^{2} O(1)$ $C(n) = O(m \log m)$ $C(n) = \sum_{i=1}^{h}\sum_{i=1}^{2} O(1)$ $C(n) = O(1)$
7.	At Sender : Data path choice	$O(g)$
8.	Step 8 Packet Creation and forwarded Step 8.1 Priority Timer() Step 8.2 Combo-Casting() Note: t1 is the time for T_{stores} timer.	$C(n) = \sum_{i=1}^{p} 1$ $C(n) = O(1) * O(t_1 + 1)*O(1)$
	TOTAL	$T(n) = O(n^2)$

Step 1.   Sender sends ECHO-packet .It takes constant time i.e. O(1) .If there are many senders exists at the same time , then parallel all the senders will send Echo Packet .

So, complexity at this step is constant i.e. O(1).

Step 2.   DMs create a Parital_Cost_Matrix . Since a pair of node is always connected via one DM. So, partial matrix will run for i=1 to i=2 and j=1 to j=2. Since at this step, we are considering only two nodes i.e. n=2.

C(n) = outer loop x inner loop

The basic operation in inner loop is compare value of 'i' and 'j', if found equal then assign the cost, as infinity; else assign some valid cost to that link. This Basic operation takes O(1) time to get complete.

$$C(n) = \sum_{i=1}^{n} \sum_{i=1}^{n} 1 \qquad ; where, \ n = 2.$$

$$= \sum_{i=1}^{n} 2 \qquad \left(\text{Using the rule} \quad \sum_{i=1}^{n} 1 = n \in O(n) \right)$$

$$= 2\sum_{i=1}^{n} 1 \quad = 2*2 = 4 = O(4)$$

So, the efficiency of RSM2 model, at step-2 is O(4).

Step 3.   DMs floods the Partial_Cost_Matrix by calling, flood _partial_ matrix( ) function.

C(n) = Outerloop x innerloop.

In this step, for loop as an outer loop and while loop as an inner loop. Since, In echo packet, sender's-id is mentioned. DMs use that id as a destination address.

In while loop, packet of partial_cost_matrix will forward from one node to next, till the sender of that echo packet found. Assignment takes O(1) time.

Let 'k' be the no. of nodes, through which packet has to pass, before reaching to its destination. So the 'while' statement executes (k+1) times. When condition is true i.e. when node is not the original sender, the execution happens tobe n-times and the statement executes when node is found as original sender. But this time operations under while-loop will not performed.

37

$$C(n) = \sum_{i=1}^{d} (k+1)$$

Step 3.1. If there is any changes occur in topology of the network, then we will backtrack to step-2. As many time, changes occurs, we will have to backtrack to step-2. So if we assume that in backtracking, we need O(1) time, then we can conclude as follows :

No. of topology updates = No. of Back-tracks to step-2.

This step is optional.

Step 3.2. Go to step-4, if topology remains unchanged.

Step 4.   At this step, Sender has to consolidate all the partial matrix, received from DRs, in to one final Cost_Matrix. So, efficiency in this case is O(nxn).

Step 5.   Efficiency of the algorithm is O(1), when one of the DM is selected by Sender, for network computations. In this way, we calculate the complexity of MCPA algorithm, i.e. quadratic in Nature.

4.1.2   Algorithm for RMTP protocol

Step 1.   Tree Construction

        {
        // n : total no. of nodes in network
            N0 ← Source Router
            i ← 0
                for(i=0;i<=n;i++)
            {
        count_child_receiver() ; // calculate the Childs and Receivers for a N_i
        // Connect the N_i to the Childs and connect the receivers to the Ni
                connect_child_receiver();
                Goto next node   // i=i+1

            }
Step 2.   Group the Routers

Group()

{

// c : no. of childs under the node.

1.Root <- N0

2. Find all the nodes of the root node.

3. For(i=0;i<c ;i++)

{

// Check whether it has any child or not.

If (has child)

Select the current node as X

Call the sub tree having X as root.

Make_group()

{

//Mark it as a group.

.}

Select_DR()

}

Step 3.   Selection of DR

Select_DR ()

{

//few specific nodes act as DR . But the choice of DR for a given local region is done dynamically.

// n : no. of nodes in tree.

for(i=1;i<=n;i++)

{

Choice_dr()

{

ttl ← 64

for (i=0 ;i < n;i++)

{

SEND_ACK_TO_ME packet sent via DR , periodically;

39

ttl = ttl – 1 ; // ttl-value decremented by one at each hope of the network

If (Largest ttl value in SEND_ACK_TO_ME packet at DR)

{

    DR   ←—NACK-processor for the node-i

}   } } }

}

Table 4.2 Complexity analysis for RMTP algorithm

Steps	Operation	Complexity
1	Tree construction	O(n)
2	Grouping of Nodes	O(c)
3	Selection Of DR	O(n)
	Total	O(n)+O(c)

4.2   Algorithmic Computations to the Network Topology

4.2.1   Exposure of RSM2 to the networks

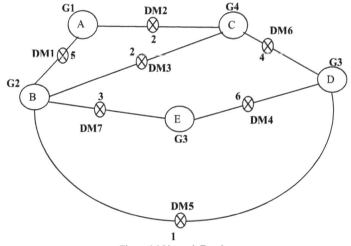

Figure 4.1 Network Topology

TOPOLOGY's DESCRIPTION

- Let each node belongs to a particular group, as shown below in the following table:

Table 4.3 Nodes with their group-identity

Node(s)	Group (G)
A	G1
B	G2
C	G4
D	G3
E	G3

Table 4.4 Dynamics Manager stores the information of nodes & cost of edges as Matrix

Dynamics Managers	Cost Matrix	EDGES
DM-1	$\begin{bmatrix} \infty & 5 \\ 5 & \infty \end{bmatrix}$	AB ,BA
DM-2	$\begin{bmatrix} \infty & 2 \\ 2 & \infty \end{bmatrix}$	AC, CA
DM-3	$\begin{bmatrix} \infty & 2 \\ 2 & \infty \end{bmatrix}$	BC, CB
DM-4	$\begin{bmatrix} \infty & 6 \\ 6 & \infty \end{bmatrix}$	ED, DE
DM-5	$\begin{bmatrix} \infty & 1 \\ 1 & \infty \end{bmatrix}$	BD, DB
DM-6	$\begin{bmatrix} \infty & 4 \\ 4 & \infty \end{bmatrix}$	CD, DC
DM-7	$\begin{bmatrix} \infty & 3 \\ 3 & \infty \end{bmatrix}$	BE, EB

- Nodes are connected through routers-collocated with Dynamics Manager. Dynamics Manager already knows the cost of the link that is directly connected to it. Each Dynamics Manager has the information about the nodes and the cost of the link, connecting them in the form of matrix as shown below:

CASE –I: Node –'A' wants to communicate with 'group-G2' and 'group-G3'.

Step 1. 'A' floods (OFA) echo packet.

Step 2. All DMs runs IGMP as, they get Echo-packet and form a Partial-cost matrix by executing step- 1 of MCPA algorithm.

Step 3. Partial-Cost matrix flooded (OFA) throughout the network.

Step 4. As, the sender gets Partial-Cost Matrix, extract the results and forms finally, a Cost-Matrix of nxn:

n: no. of nodes in the network

$$
C[i][j] \;=\;
\begin{bmatrix}
 & A & B & C & D & E \\
A & \infty & 5 & 2 & \infty & \infty \\
B & 5 & \infty & 2 & 1 & 3 \\
C & 2 & \infty & \infty & 4 & \infty \\
D & \infty & 1 & 4 & \infty & 6 \\
E & \infty & 3 & \infty & 6 & \infty
\end{bmatrix}
$$

Figure 4.2 Cost-Matrix created at the Sender's site

42

Step 5.   Let node 'A' chooses DM-1, for the next Network computational activities.

$$\begin{bmatrix} Edges & \cos t \\ AB & 5 \\ AC & 2 \\ BC & 2 \\ BE & 3 \\ BD & 1 \\ CD & 4 \\ DE & 6 \end{bmatrix} \quad \text{After applying-Sort} \Longrightarrow \quad \begin{bmatrix} Edges & \cos t \\ BD & 1 \\ AC & 2 \\ BC & 2 \\ BE & 3 \\ CD & 4 \\ AB & 5 \\ DE & 6 \end{bmatrix}$$

Work-Matrix   Sorted Work-Matrix

Figure 4.3 Sorted Work-Matrix

Step 5.1. DM-1 creates a Work matrix by executing step - 2 of MCPA algorithm. Then applies step-3, and get sorted Work-Matrix by heap-sort.

Step 5.2. DM -1 uses the results of Step-5.1 and constructs a Priority-Matrix by executing the step-4 of MCPA algorithm.

$$\begin{bmatrix} Edges & \text{Pr} iority \\ BD & 1 \\ AC & 2 \\ BC & 2 \\ BE & 3 \end{bmatrix}$$

Figure 4.4 Priority-Matrix

Step 5.3. DM-1 sends the Priority Matrix to node-'A'. Since, Node-A already has the IGMP status report, so it creates a Data-delivery path for the Nodes (i.e. B, D and E), belonging to 'group-2' and 'group-3'.

Step 6.   Data is delivered as shown in figure 4.7

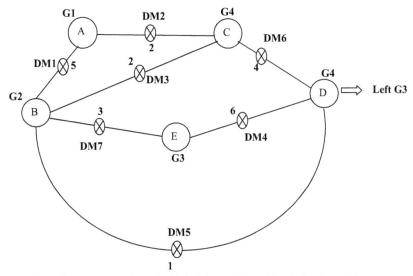

Figure 4.5 Network Topology after Node-D Leaves Group-G3 and Joins Group G4

CASE –II: Node –'A' wants to communicate with 'group-G2' and 'group-G3'. But node-D immediately leaves 'group-3' and joining 'group-4'.

Step 1.   'A' floods (OFA) echo packet.

Step 2.   All DMs runs IGMP as, they get Echo-packet and form a Partial-cost matrix by executing step- 1 of MCPA algorithm.

Step 3.   Partial-Cost matrix flooded (OFA) throughout the network.

Step 4.   As the sender gets Partial-Cost Matrix, extracts the results and forms finally a Cost-Matrix of nxn, n: no. of nodes in the network.

$$C[i][j] \;=\; \begin{bmatrix} & A & B & C & D & E \\ A & \infty & 5 & 2 & \infty & \infty \\ B & 5 & \infty & 2 & 1 & 3 \\ C & 2 & \infty & \infty & 4 & \infty \\ D & \infty & 1 & 4 & \infty & 6 \\ E & \infty & 3 & \infty & 6 & \infty \end{bmatrix}$$

Figure 4.6 Partial Cost-Matrix created at the Dynamic Manager's site

Step 5.   Suddenly, as the sender gets matrix, Host-D leaves group-3 and joins group-4. Host- D will send a leave-report before leaving the group.

Step 6.   DM updates its cost matrix and floods (optimized) immediately to all.

Step 7.   Sender get that report will update the path and send the data.

Step 8.   Data is delivered as shown below.

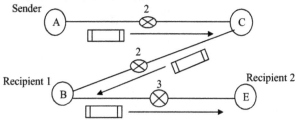

Figure 4.7 Node –'A' wants to communicate with 'group-G2' and 'group-G3'

CHAPTER - 5   IMPLEMENTATION OF MCPA ALGORITHM

In this chapter we have some snapshots that show the implementation results of MCPA algorithm, which has been designed to describe RSM2. For the implementation of MCPA algorithm, we opt 'C' as coding language.

The description of each snapshot is given below:

- Snapshot 1: This snapshot has taken, when the topology is decided by the user and she assigns the cost to each link of the same network. It is depicted in Figure 5.1 and Figure 5.2, deciding the topology of network and assigning the cost by User.
- Snapshot 2: This snapshot has taken, when the main steps of the algorithm comes into action. It shows the formation of Cost-Matrix, Sorted Work Matrix and Priority Matrix using the data that has been entered by the user in Snapshot 1. It is depicted in Figure 5.2, Formation of Cost-Matrix, Sorted Work Matrix & Priority Matrix.
- Snapshot 3: This snapshot has taken, when the user decides which group to be allocated to each node. It is depicted inFigure 5.3 Each node is assigned to the specific group , as entered by user.
- Snapshot 4: This snapshot has taken, when the user has been asked to decide the sender node. In RSM2 model, we can have more than one node as Sender(s). Along with it, user tells with how many groups, he wants to communicate as receiver(s). It is depicted in Figure 5.5, Sender Node and Receiver group is entered by user.
- Snapshot 5: This snapshot has taken, when Sender finds out the Priority Matrix and uses that path to send the data. It is depicted in Figure 5.4 Senders(S) use Priority Matrix to send the Data to Desirable Receivers(R).

5.1 SNAPSHOTS

```
C:\TC\A3.EXE                                          _ 5 X

Enter number of nodes
5
Want to enter weight from node 1 to 2
Enter 1 to assign weight
1

Enter weight := 21
Want to enter weight from node 1 to 3
Enter 1 to assign weight
1

Enter weight := 10
Want to enter weight from node 1 to 4
Enter 1 to assign weight
1

Enter weight := 29
Want to enter weight from node 1 to 5
Enter 1 to assign weight
1

Enter weight := 30
```

Figure 5.1 Deciding the topology of network and assigning the cost by User.

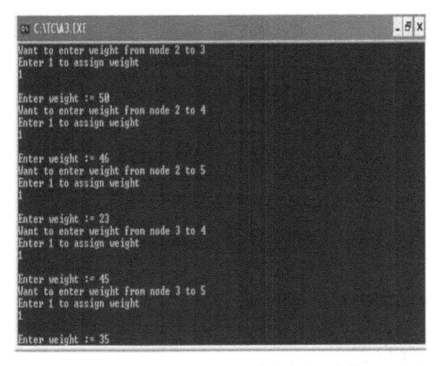

Figure 5.2 Deciding the topology of network and assigning the cost by User.

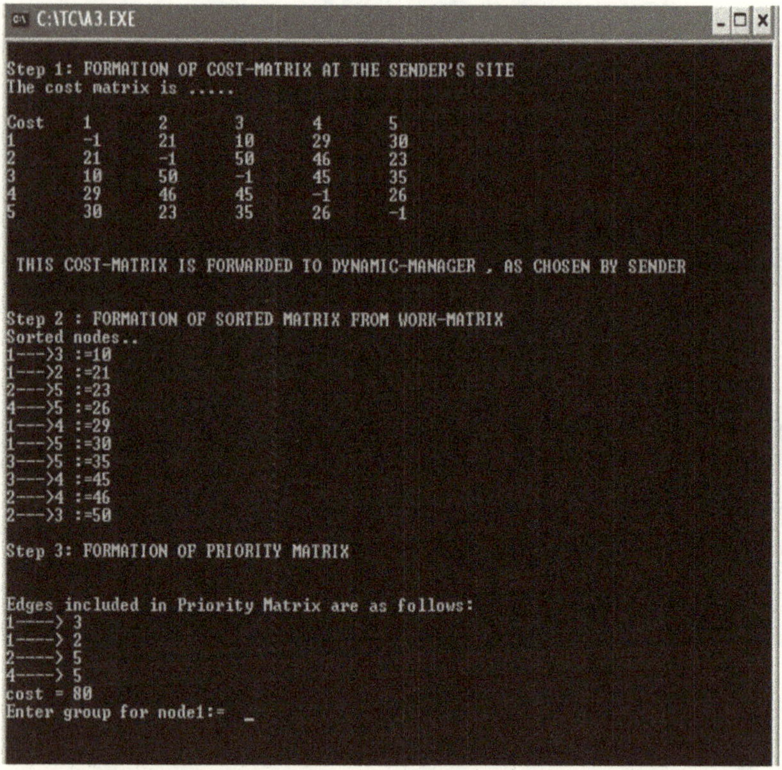

```
C:\TC\A3.EXE                                                    _□x

Step 1: FORMATION OF COST-MATRIX AT THE SENDER'S SITE
The cost matrix is .....

Cost    1       2       3       4       5
1       -1      21      10      29      30
2       21      -1      50      46      23
3       10      50      -1      45      35
4       29      46      45      -1      26
5       30      23      35      26      -1


 THIS COST-MATRIX IS FORWARDED TO DYNAMIC-MANAGER , AS CHOSEN BY SENDER


Step 2 : FORMATION OF SORTED MATRIX FROM WORK-MATRIX
Sorted nodes..
1--->3 :=10
1--->2 :=21
2--->5 :=23
4--->5 :=26
1--->4 :=29
1--->5 :=30
3--->5 :=35
3--->4 :=45
2--->4 :=46
2--->3 :=50

Step 3: FORMATION OF PRIORITY MATRIX


Edges included in Priority Matrix are as follows:
1---> 3
1---> 2
2---> 5
4---> 5
cost = 80
Enter group for node1:=  _
```

Figure 5.3 Formation of Cost-Matrix , Sorted Work Matrix & Priority Matrix.

```
 C:\TCVA3.EXE                                          - □ ×
2        21      -1      50      46      23        Maximi
3        10      50      -1      45      35
4        29      46      45      -1      26
5        30      23      35      26      -1

   THIS COST-MATRIX IS FORWARDED TO DYNAMIC-MANAGER , AS CHOSEN BY SENDER

Step 2 : FORMATION OF SORTED MATRIX FROM WORK-MATRIX
Sorted nodes..
1--->3 :=10
1--->2 :=21
2--->5 :=23
4--->5 :=26
1--->4 :=29
1--->5 :=30
3--->5 :=35
3--->4 :=45
2--->4 :=46
2--->3 :=50

Step 3: FORMATION OF PRIORITY MATRIX

Edges included in Priority Matrix are as follows:
1----> 3
1----> 2
2----> 5
4----> 5
cost = 80
Enter group for node1:=  g1

Enter group for node2:=  g2

Enter group for node3:=  g3

Enter group for node4:=  g4

Enter group for node5:=  g1
```

Figure 5.4 Each node is assigned to the specific group , as entered by user

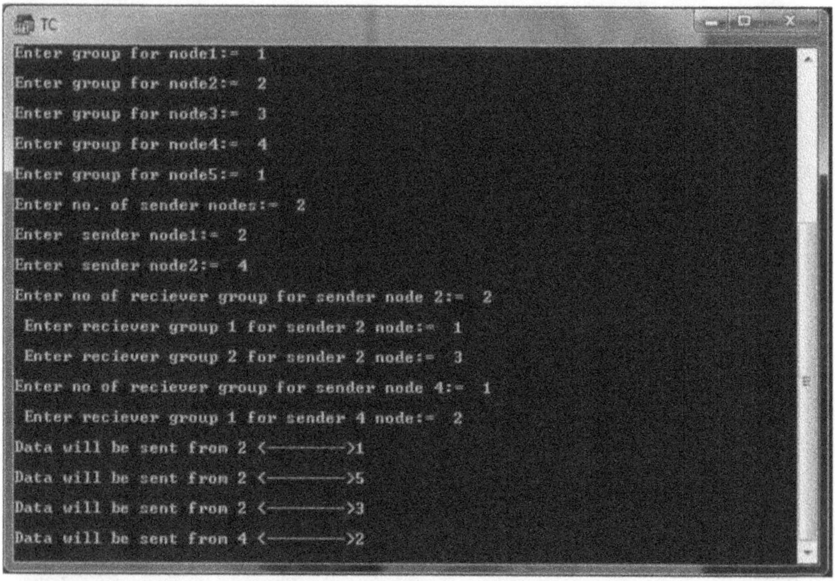

Figure 5.5 Sender Node and Receiver group is entered by user

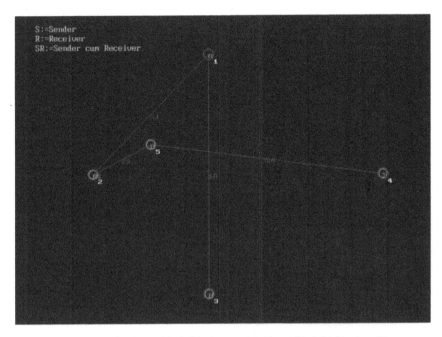

Figure 5.6 Senders(S) use Priority Matrix to send the Data to Desirable Receivers(R)

CHAPTER - 6   COMPARISON OF RSM2 WITH RMTP

There is a wealth of literature on reliable multicasting. Several new papers have also appeared in the recent literature that focuses on Wide Area networks [4] describes the design of Reliable Multicast Transport Protocol that uses efficient local-recovery technique for serving the missing packets.

Our work is closely related to RMTP, with significant differences .Let us study in details the comparative study of RSM2 over RMTP.

[1] Design: RSM2 opt flat design approach while RMTP works on hierarchical design. Flat design facilitates RSM2 to work in all the kinds of situation i.e.

a) One-to –Many:

RSM2 fits in the situation, where one sender communicates with many receivers on the network. RMTP is also good in this scenario.

b) Many –to-Many:

RSM2 fits in this situation, where many senders want to starts communication at the same time. RMTP does not fit in this scenario, it opts hierarchical approach, and in hierarchical, at one time only one node is the root of that hierarchy, i.e. the original sender.

c) ALL-to-ALL:

RSM2 fits in this situation, where all the nodes at the network want to go in communication, with each other. Flat design approach facilitates to work in all the three scenarios. In flat design, there is no root and no leaf. RMTP again does not fit in this scenario because of its hierarchical design. Since as the number of senders will start the communication, simultaneously, then a dilemma will occur about, who will be the root of that hierarchy.

53

[2] Best Path:

RSM2 provides best path for the packet delivery. RSM2 use Kruskal's Algorithm for minimum spanning path, to reach to the all presentable nodes on the network. This path is further reduced if it includes some undesirable nodes. So, the data-packet is transmitted over short path, with minimum cost .But, in RMTP these concepts are not introduced. In RMTP, data is just multicasted without concerning cost or delay of the links, and the responsibility of sender is transferred to DR, i.e. Designated Receiver.

[3] Dynamics Co-operativity:

RSM2 model is designed in such a way, to work in dynamics also. RSM2 works well in Wired Networks and in Infrastructure Wireless Networks also. Working of RSM2 in Infrastructure - less Wireless Networks is the part of future scope. Hence, RSM2 is capable to co-operate dynamics well. RMTP works well in static environment only and do not cooperate well with dynamics of nodes. Since, in RMTP designated receivers are chosen statically, based on approximate location of receivers. So it halts in wireless networks. Hence, RMTP does not provide Dynamic Cooperativity.

[4] Combo-Casting:

RSM2 use Combo-Casting to serve NACKs hence reduces duplication of packets effectively. Dynamic Managers first stores all the NACKs, and wait for a random amount of time, T_{NACK}. As, the time gets out DMs decide either to retransmit the data through multicasting or via unicasting. If more NACKs are received for the same packet then DM subgroups them into a new group and multicast the missed data-packet. In case, there is one or two nodes send NACK for the same packet, then, DMs unicast the missed data packet.

In RMTP, Designated Receiver buffers the packet and if NACK comes for a missing packet, then it is first served by the DR, who is looking after that area .If this DR, becomes unable to serve that request, and then request will go to its Parent DR and so on. Finally reach to the sender, if no DR serves that request.

[5] Reliability & Scalability:

The objective of our Model-RSM2 in this thesis is to guarantee *reliability* achieving high throughput, maintaining low end-to-end delay. This is achieved by reducing unnecessary retransmissions by the sender.

[6] Load on Sender:

RSM2 put fewer loads on Sender, because the load has been shifted from Sender node to Dynamic Managers.

[7] DMs Vs. DRs:

DMs have high network-computations ability for all network computations like – to create the priority matrix and updates the matrix, whenever the node topology changes.

[8] Retransmissions:

In RSM2 model, we use Combo-casting technique for the retransmission purpose, to deal with lost-packets.

[9] Complexity:

Complexity of RSM2 is O (nxn) but Complexity of RMTP is O (n).
Complexity of RSM2 > Complexity of RMTP
$$O (n \times n) > O (n)$$

6.1 Graph shows a relation between Cost of the link and time for packets Buffering

As per the comparative analysis of algorithm designed for RSM2 and algorithm designed for RMTP, we found that complexity of RSM2 is quadratic in nature, while, complexity of RMTP is linear.

Let us study the following graph , which shows us a pattern between cost of the link and the time foe packets buffering. In RSM2 , we have introduced a new concept that for the link having high

55

cost , we need much larger time to buffer the packet for that link. This relation has been shown in the graph.

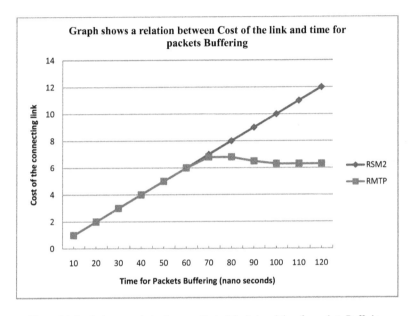

Figure 6.1 Graph shows a relation between Cost of the link and time for packets Buffering

CHAPTER - 7   CONCLUSION AND FUTURE SCOPE

Wireless networks are an emerging new technology that will allow users to access information and services electronically, regardless of their geographic position. Wireless networks can be classified in two types.

Infrastructure network: Such a kind of wireless networks comprises of a network with fixed and wired gateways. The hosts are mobile .The mobile unit can move geographically during the communication. When it goes out of range of one base station, it connects with new base station and starts communicating through it. This is called handoff .In this approach base-station are fixed [5].

Infrastructure less (adhoc) networks: In contrast to infrastructure-based networks, in adhoc networks all the nodes are mobile and can be connected dynamically in an arbitrary manner. All nodes of these networks behave as routers and take part in discovery and maintenance of routes to other nodes in the network.

It is concluded that RSM2 can be implemented in wireless i.e., Infrastuctured Network, unlike RMTP, if capability and computability of RSM2 is applied over Base-station. Along with it, RSM2 works easily in dynamic environment where more than one sender sends data simultaneously, unlike RMTP. A node can act as Sender and Receiver both at the same time simultaneously, unlike RMTP. If one node leaves the topology, then DMs update its Partial matrix and forwards this information to the sender and other nodes periodically. Hence, RSM2 can also be applied to hybrid networks also. This is the part for future research.

Limitation of this Model is that, it's set-up cost is greater and cannot be established for Infrastructure less (adhoc) Networks. As the number of users increases, the cost to implement this model also get increases.

REFERENCES

[1]   Ali Alsaih and Tariq Alahdal, "Non-Real Time Reliable Multicast Protocol Using Sub-Sub Casting," *The International Arab Journal of Information Technology*, Vol. 4, No.1, January 2007.

[2]   Tie Liao, "Light-weight Reliable Multicast Protocol", *INRIA*, Rocquencourt, BP 105, 78153 Le Chesnay Cedex, France.

[3]   Danyang Zhang, Sibabrata Ray, Rajgopal Kannan, S. Sitharama Iyengar "A Recovery Algorithm for Reliable Multicasting in reliable networks." Proceedings of the 2003 *International Conference on Parallel Processing* (ICPP'03).

[4]   Sanjoy Paul, Member, IEEE, Krishna K. Sabnani, Fellow, IEEE, John C.-H. Lin and Supratik Bhattacharyya "Reliable Multicast Transport Protocol (RMTP)". *IEEE journal on Selected Areas in Communications*, Vol. 15, No. 3, April 1997.

[5]   K.K.Singh, Akansha Singh,"Mobile Computing", *Umesh Publications.*

[6]   Behrouz A Forouzan, "Data Communications and Networking", Fourth Edition.

[7]   http://www.differencebetween.com/difference-between-flooding-and-vs-broadcasting/

[8]   Carolos Livadas, Idit Keidar, Nancy A. Lynch "Designing a Caching-Based Reliable Multicast Protocol".

[9]   Adamson, C. Bormann, M. Handley, J. Macker "NACK-Oriented Reliable Multicast (NORM) Transport Protocol".

[10]   Wei yang, Wanlu Sun, Linhuali, "Reliable Multicasting for Device-to-Device Radio Underlying Cellular Networks" , 4 March,2012.

[11]   Luo Junhai, Xue Liu, Ye Daxia, "Research on Multicast Routing Protocols for Mobile Ad-hoc Networks" , Elsevier, 2007

PUBLICATION

Published a Research Paper on "A Reliable & Scalable Multicast Model"(RSM2), in International Journal of Recent Technology and Engineering (IJRTE) ISSN: 2277-3878, Volume-1, Issue-2

Abstract— Multicasting is the ability of a communication network to accept a single message from an application and to deliver copies of the message to multiple recipients at different location [1]. With the emergence of mobile users, many existing Internet - protocols, including those with multicast support, need to be adapted in order to offer support to this increasingly growing class of users. Our research in multicasting, as to design a Multicast Model, which provides reliability & scalability with best path for data delivery. Reliability means guaranteed Delivery of packets. Scalability means capability to serve growing needs .In this context , A few concepts of Proactive routing technique are used to make available this model in Infrastructured wireless also. Minimum Spanning path is used to deliver the packets, to reduce the cost & delay.